College Can Wait!

*The reluctant student's guide to
gap years, resume-building, travel, internships,
and figuring out what you really want*

R.J. VICKERS

*This book is dedicated to Sam, Josh, Daniel,
and all of the other young people out there
who wish they had a second option.*

Introduction

It's been a long journey to reach this point. Soon you'll leave high school behind and venture into the scary unknown called the Real World.

And as soon as you graduate, everyone assumes you will attend college.

If you're experiencing doubts at this point, you're far from alone. The world expects you to get a prestigious degree, enter the business world, and become "successful." Meanwhile, you're worried about what to wear for prom and whether you'll fail Chemistry. And when you think about it, you don't really like the idea of four more years of school.

In fact, you hate it.

But it's expected of you.

The problem is, college has become the *only* respectable option for students straight out of high school. Anything else constitutes failure. You've spent years honing your grades, taking on more and more AP classes, and studying for the SATs and ACTs. College has been emphasized as the be-all, end-all to success and financial stability.

Yet it's no longer a good option for everyone. Costs are rising. Graduate studies are becoming necessary to secure a job. Recent graduates are forced to move back in with their parents as they search fruitlessly for work. When you enter college, you may be signing yourself up for a lifetime of debt.

What's the solution to this conundrum? It's simpler than you might expect.

Don't go to college.

Not yet, anyway.

If you don't know what to major in; if you're torn between two majors; if you can't stand the thought of any more school—don't do it! It's that simple.

But it's also one of the most difficult decisions you could possibly make.

You'll face pressure from your parents, your teachers, and your peers.

You'll face disappointment and worry.

But if you read this book, you'll see why choosing a different route is just as valid as going straight to college. Outside the classroom, you'll find happiness, independence, and even education. You'll become a more interesting person, a better-rounded person, and a more conscientious member of society. If you do go back to college, you'll be ready to make the most of the opportunity. And if you don't, you'll never mistake a degree for "success" again.

THE BEST UNIVERSITY STUDENT

As the daughter of a university professor, I've heard countless stories about the best and worst students in class. Again and again, I've heard about the freshman who doesn't attend class, flunks her tests, and doesn't turn in assignments (she has an endless roster of dead grandmothers whose funerals she *must* attend whenever one is due, of course), wasting her education because she isn't ready for it. That's a huge waste of money and time.

Don't be that student.

Instead, be my mother's best student—a 27-year-old man who spent most of his twenties living in a tent on a beach, surfing and growing dreadlocks, before returning to university to excel at his major.

Or be the young woman who ditches college to live the life her friends can only dream of. That was me...sort of. Though I did graduate from my university, I spent my summers and semesters off traveling, working abroad, and generally having a great time—which served me much better than my degree in the long term.

Trust me—I've seen it a hundred times. You can travel, earn money, and live a fulfilling life entirely without a college degree.

SHOULD YOU CONSIDER SOMETHING ELSE?

This book could be just the escape route you've been looking for. See if this sounds like you:

- Are you unsure of what to study?
- Do you feel pressured to choose a major that isn't right for you?
- Are you fed up with school?
- Do you dread the idea of another 4 years of study?
- Do you want to escape? To travel? To try something new?
- Are you afraid you might hate the career you've chosen?
- Do you feel directionless?
- Do you feel like a disappointment to your family, teachers, or peers?

If you agree with one or more of these points, you should seriously consider taking time out to see what you really want before you decide to attend university.

If you hate the idea of college, I'll convince you that it might not be right for you. I'll show you every alternative option you've never heard of—the travel secrets and thrilling jobs and alternative paths that no one talks about. And I'll give you a list of talking points you can use to get your parents and friends on board.

Be warned: you are about to break out of the system. You'll be a rebel.

Some people might never come to terms with that. If those people include your parents, it might hurt. They want nothing but the best for you. They want you to be successful and happy. Sadly, they don't realize that they're mistaking *high-level degree* for *success* and *prestige* for *happiness*. There are many different types of success, just as there are endless routes to happiness.

Read on to learn the secrets to finding your fun, fulfilling non-college path. Remember, you can always return and study later, once you know what you want. But right now, university is looming, and you have to make your decision soon. Don't gamble the best years of your life on a degree that won't pay off.

Take a chance *now*.

SECTION I

College Isn't Everything

What if college isn't for you?

This is probably something you haven't seen before—a book designed to persuade you *not* to attend college. But it should be obvious that college isn't for everyone, and even those who do need to study might not benefit from it straight out of high school. In this chapter, I'll turn your preconceived notions of college, success, and life after high school upside down. You'll see that there is much more to life than fitting yourself into the most acceptable mold.

The simple truth is, you'll only get as much out of college as you put into it. So if you aren't ready or you don't want it, there's no point in going. It's a major waste of time and money. Ideally, college should give you the freedom to pursue the career you desire. In truth, it often traps you with crippling debts that can haunt you for the rest of your life.

If this doesn't make you think twice, what will?

It's common to see university freshmen who take advantage of their newfound freedom by skipping classes, staying up all night partying, and generally having a great time. While this is a great time for you to explore your bounds, it's just as easy to do this without taking on $20,000 of debt for the experience. You'd be much better off traveling, working, or just getting away from home to test your independence in a less burdensome way. Once you've decided you're ready to get started on a degree, you can choose a university that suits your purposes, focus on the major that's right for you, and get the most you can out of the experience.

Furthermore, if you're stuck between two majors, you would be better off trying out various jobs that interest you, rather than switching back and forth between majors and prolonging your education (unless that's what you want!). I've heard from countless students who have been forced to choose a completely random major just so they could graduate on time, which serves no one.

And if you decide college isn't for you, you'll avoid wasting your (or your parents') hard-earned money, not to mention the best years of your life, on something that you never wanted.

Besides, most majors are a waste of money anyway. As anyone who has studied literature, philosophy, math, or non-medical psychology can tell you, these classes prepare you to teach those subjects—and not much else. If you don't like the idea of teaching, there isn't much reason to pursue a subject with no other job opportunities. And while teaching is a perfectly respectable profession, it doesn't pay well. If your idea of success involves making a good income, you probably aren't dreaming of a steady teaching job.

For instance, one young man earned a degree in philosophy (widely regarded as one of the most useless majors!) and quickly entered a fun, lucrative stint as a ski instructor. Many years down the road, he was back at school—this time teaching English.

STOP BEFORE YOU'RE BROKE

But you could do much worse than earn yourself a useless degree.

Under the guidance of many well-meaning teachers and parents, you could take out a bundle of student loans to finance your education...and realize, years down the line, that you don't have any hope of paying them off.

Ever.

That has become the grim reality for college students across the US. Worst of all, this is a problem that's unique to the States. Students in Japan and Europe and Australia often grumble about the price of tuition, but they expect to pay no more than $5,000 a semester. Some lucky students even get free college tuition nationwide (in Scotland, for instance). When they hear that American students are paying $20,000 or even $50,000 a year, they're utterly shocked. College in the US has been blown completely out of proportion. We grow up thinking it's normal to pay as much for college as you would for your first home, when in all reality, the usefulness of a college degree has declined while the price tag has soared.

And what happens after you graduate, saddled with debt and a very fancy degree?

You either go to graduate school...or you move back in with your parents.

Because an undergraduate degree will not prepare you for a job. Very few do. If you want to be a doctor, you'll have 4 more years of school to complete. If you want to study law, you have to go to law school. Even a degree in writing (the least guaranteed of fields you'll find!) will take another 4 years of study.

Once you move back in with your parents, you'll take an unpaid internship that gives you a foot into the door of your desired industry, or you'll settle for a low-level job unrelated to your major. (Engineers and business majors might be the lone exception to this). The importance of a college degree has been so over-emphasized in the US that we have an abundance of intellectuals and not enough jobs to take them all. What the US really needs is people to fill the necessary jobs.

This country needs plumbers. Electricians. Mechanics. Cooks. Builders. But a college degree won't get you any of these jobs. No; unless you're extremely lucky, you'll resign yourself to flipping burgers until something better comes along. If it ever does.

Does this sound like fun?

Are you excited to take on crippling amounts of debt with no promise of payoff?

I have several friends who left college with over $200,000 of debt. Yikes! And I know a few others who have already resigned themselves to the fact that they'll never pay off their student loans.

One has even made plans never to earn enough to be forced to start paying off his loans. He's resigned himself to an eternity of living near minimum wage. Yet it's better than trying to dig himself out of debt.

Debt is a big, ugly reality of studying these days, but as long as students continue to line up and cough up their fees, colleges will continue to charge extortionate amounts. If you don't want to study, or if you don't have any idea of what to major in, the smartest thing you can do is *stay away from college*. Do something else. Get out of your parents' house. Move away. Experience the world. Explore your independence.

If moving out sounds like an intimidating prospect, meet me in Section 2 for a life-changing list of non-college ideas.

THE DARK SIDE OF LOVING PARENTAL PRESSURE

There is one final reason why college might be the wrong choice for you, and this one is a bit uglier. The truth is, if you don't want to go to college, the **worst possible thing** your parents can do is force it upon you.

Early adulthood is a very difficult, uncertain time of life. Even if you love the path you've chosen and have a supportive group of friends by your side, you'll experience growing pains. Independence is harder than it looks. Some days you'll love staying out until sunrise and passing out on your friend's couch, and other days you'll wish more than anything that you could just curl up with your puppy at home and gobble down a plate of your favorite homemade chocolate-chip cookies.

And if you've chosen your degree because it made your parents happy (which, as depressing as it sounds, is true of a more than half of the students I've known), you might resent them for pushing you into a difficult program—and, at the same time, feel worthless when you don't live up to their expectations. I've known students who have flunked out of college and moved back in with their parents, so miserable they barely left the house. And I know one student who committed suicide because the pressures of college were too overwhelming.

If your parents have pushed you and pushed you, they never know when they might just push you over the edge. They are not doing you any kindness.

As you approach your twenties, the fear of disappointing your parents is still a major factor in your life. It's going to take a lot of courage to break free from the mold of "what my parents want," and you might get a lot of grief for it, but it's best to free yourself from your parents' expectations **now**. Like ripping off a band-aid, it's easier if you do it quickly and easily, rather than drawing out the process for years.

Stop and think about it.

If you choose a major because your parents want it, they'll expect you to pursue a job in that field.

If you land a job in that field, your parents will expect you to become successful, which means remaining there for years and working your way up the ranks.

And they'll expect you to stay there.

When you look back at the age of 50, you'll realize that you have just wasted half of your life working at a job you hate, simply because your parents expected it of you. It sounds ludicrous, but it happens all the time. The fear of disappointing those you love is powerful and unrelenting.

One woman I'll call Lisa went to medical school and worked as a surgeon until she was in her 50s. She hated her job. At long last, Lisa quit her job and became a pastry chef, which was something she had always dreamed of. When her mother heard the news, she disowned her.

The point is, no matter how many years of your life you pour into filling someone else's image of success, you might never satisfy them. Do you want to live your life based on that impossible goal?

Or do you want to live the life *you* want?

* * *

Now you've seen why college might not be the best answer for you, at least not yet. Some of your preconceived notions have been questioned—no, it's not an economically sound idea to invest big in an education that you don't want and might not pay off—and you've seen why settling into a career path you don't want will haunt you years down the road.

The next chapter will tempt you still further to look past college—I'll persuade you that your twenties are one of the freest times of your life, and show you why you ought to take advantage of that freedom.

Your moment of freedom

If you've reached this point in the book, you've realized that there are a number of entirely valid reasons to delay college—or to forgo it entirely. On top of that, your twenties is the ideal time to explore—to get out there and experience the world, and to figure out what you really want out of life. It's not necessarily the ideal time to be trapped in a classroom, doing exactly what you've been doing for the past 12 years of your life.

If you're even a bit hesitant about starting college, take my advice: use your freedom wisely.

You'll never be as free as you are in your twenties. You have the chance to leave home, so you'll soon be tasting your first years of complete independence; meanwhile, the realities of adult life haven't quite caught up with you yet. You don't have a job tying you down, nor do you have debt, a mortgage to pay off, or kids to look after. You probably don't even have a partner or spouse.

The world is your oyster. If you don't take advantage of this opportunity now, you'll look back in ten years and realize that you lost your chance at freedom. So seize the moment. Go forth and conquer!

A KICK OUT THE DOOR

Here's my first piece of advice: **leave home**.

It doesn't matter where you go. Even college freshman who move into a dorm five minutes away from their parents' house get their first experience of independence. If you want to move to a different state or travel abroad, that's wonderful too. The point is to get out.

Once you're away from home, you'll realize something funny— the more physical distance you put between yourself and your parents, the less power their opinions have over you. Even if they've been supportive and loving from day one, you'll think differently once you're alone. I was one of the lucky teens whose parents (both with Master's degrees) fully supported the idea of delaying or skipping college. Yet even they exerted a subtle sort of pressure on me. They always believed me to be a shy, quiet kid, so they often encouraged me to speak out and interact with others.

Instead, I rebelled and turned quieter than ever.

It was only once I was living alone, working and traveling in fantastic places, that I realized I was actually quite a social person. If I had stayed at home, I would never have left my comfort zone. I would have been the quiet one forever.

My mother took the idea of "leaving home" to the other extreme. You see, once you're away from your parents, you can do whatever you want, and they can't do a thing to stop you. After high school, my mother took a year off to live with a host family in Japan, intending to apply for colleges from abroad. Her parents lived in California at the time, and they told her she could apply for any University of California school *except* UC Berkeley. Why? Because it was too liberal, and they were afraid she'd turn into a hippie!

Once in Japan, she applied for exactly one college: Berkeley.

She got in, and had a great time, and her parents forgave her radical tendencies.

You can shock your parents too. If you're biking around Asia or working at a vineyard in France, all those opinions and pressures that meant so much to you back home recede to nothing. Alone, you define what matters. Your priorities emerge, and you begin to understand what happiness might mean for you.

Besides, you're young. Unless you do something so stupid that you end up dead or in jail, you can just start over. This is the time to make mistakes, to act crazy, to try something extreme.

If you decide in a few years that college might be right for you after all, don't worry. It will still be waiting for you.

Your youth won't wait.

TRAVEL WHILE YOU STILL CAN!

Travel is one of the biggest perks of your twenties. Don't miss out! The idea that travel is a reward for hard work—something that should be saved for retirement—is utterly wrong. One of my favorite quotes reflects on "The most dangerous risk of all—the risk of spending your life not doing what you want on the bet that you can buy yourself the freedom to do it later" (Randy Komisar).

In other words, travel while you still can. Don't wait until you're older. Most of all, don't put it off until retirement. Traveling once you're older is completely different than traveling when you're young. You won't be climbing any mountains, you certainly won't be partying all night, and you won't be carefree enough to change plans on a whim and chase whatever adventure beckons.

One of the most exciting parts about travelling while you're young is that you'll be surrounded by your peers. Most of the people you find at hostels across Europe, Asia, Australia, and even South America are twenty-something travelers who have taken a break from their responsibilities back home to see the world. You'll be in excellent company.

If that doesn't convince you, there are several fantastic opportunities abroad that are only available for young travelers. Youth hostels, for instance, often have an age limit. More importantly, working holiday visas—more on these later— usually have a cutoff at thirty years of age.

When you feel burdened by the pressure of expectations, be sure to weigh your options carefully. Though college has become the only acceptable choice in the eyes of many, it is not a decision that should be taken lightly. If you have doubts, stop and think about it.

Do you want to take on a lifetime of debt in pursuit of a degree that means more to your parents than to you?

Or do you want to travel the world—without worrying about money?

If that sounds tempting, read on to learn about a few little-known opportunities that can change your life. You'll have the chance to earn a good income, get a taste of independence, and travel the world.

And if you're college-bound but unable to settle on a major, you'll find ideas that will help you weed out the jobs you actually hate...and settle on something that truly matters to you.

SECTION 2

A World of Possibilities

Two opposite directions

If you're considering delaying or forgoing college, it's probably for one of two reasons:

1. You have no idea what to study, or are stuck between choices

2. You don't want to study

If you don't know which career or major to go with, you would be smart to dip your toes in and try out different options. Studying a subject is nothing like working a job related to that subject, and it's good to realize that before you devote several years of your life to pursuing a set career. My mother, for instance, used to have dreams of becoming a nurse. She was intelligent, well-organized, and keen on helping people. But when she decided to volunteer in the surgical ward one summer, she nearly passed out at the sight of blood.

Imagine if she had spent four years studying nursing before she realized she could never work as a nurse!

The second half of this section will supply you with a wide range of options you can use to test out your potential careers before diving headlong into study.

However, even if you're a born academic torn between medical school and law school, you don't have to devote yourself to a year's worth of internships to choose the right path. No matter what sort of future you envision for yourself—or how directionless you feel—you might need some time to figure out what you *really* want.

And one of the best ways to do that is to travel.

See the world. Work whatever jobs catch your eye. Take chances. Meet new people. Learn more than you ever could in a classroom.

Once you return—if you ever do—you'll be a completely different person.

Best of all, you'll understand yourself in a way high school career-matching tests never could (I distinctly remember getting "clown" as my second-best career fit, while a friend of mine was best suited to becoming an aboriginal elder!).

If travel sounds daunting to you, or it seems like something completely beyond your reach, this first part is for you.

I'll show you how to travel without money, or with a tiny budget. I'll even show you how to earn more on a trip than you spend! And once you've saved a bit, I'll give you advice on how to embark on your very first solo adventure.

When I told my friends that I was heading to Europe alone for a month-long trip at the age of nineteen, most of them thought I was crazy. People questioned my parents' judgment in allowing me to do something so reckless. But I went anyway, and later followed that with a half-year in New Zealand, two more months in Europe, and a month in South America.

I came out of that experience changed forever. I could never go back to the person I was before, and I would never want to.

Even if you've never thought of traveling, making the decision to embark on a new adventure will open up your future in ways you've never imagined. So whether you're lost or just stalling, I encourage you to take advantage of the freedom of your twenties and see the world. Get out there and figure out what you really want.

It will change your life.

The first half of this section will open you up to the possibility of travel—no matter how much money or experience you have. I'll show you why getting away from home is the most important first step along your journey to adulthood, and why figuring out what you *really* want is more important than settling straightaway on a "respectable" career path.

Once you've gotten used to your independence, the second half (chapters 6 and 7) will set you back on the career path. You'll learn how to explore job options and to see what careers feel right to you...before you settle on a major. After all, a huge roster of secure, well-paying jobs don't require a college degree. And if you do decide to go back to college, you'll have a stellar resume behind you, which can win you admission and scholarships at your ideal school.

Travel, travel, travel!

MAYBE YOU DON'T CONSIDER YOURSELF A TRAVELER.

Maybe you do, but you haven't struck out on your own yet.

Either way, you'll probably find an option in this section that appeals to you. Unless you have no aspirations aside from settling down next door to your parents and helping run the family business, you're probably drawn to the idea of travel, whether you dream of soaking up the sun on white-sand beaches or practicing your French in the cafes of Paris.

There are many reasons people don't travel, but they mostly boil down to three main issues:

1. Lack of money
2. Lack of time
3. Fear

I'll address each of these limitations in this section. Be assured—no matter how broke or nervous you are, there's a way for you to see the world. And when you're young, you have nothing but time. Don't wait until it's too late to travel.

WHAT IF I'M BROKE?

Money is one of the most common reasons we *don't* travel. And it makes sense. When you have kids to raise, a mortgage to pay off, groceries to buy, and a car to maintain, adding an extra several thousand dollars to your monthly bill seems like an impossible feat.

But when you've just finished high school, you don't have to worry about any of that yet. Even if you have exactly zero money saved, at least you aren't tied to any monthly payments. You can't fully appreciate that freedom until it's gone.

How do you travel for free...without joining the Peace Corps?

You work while you're traveling.

A GATEWAY TO ADVENTURE

I'll let you on in a little secret—if you're an American, there is a fantastic website called **CoolWorks** that lists every job in the US with an awesome location. There are many in Alaska and Hawaii, and the jobs frequently involve working in or near a national park. Some are just at remote mountain ranches, and others are at ski fields and lodges and rafting companies spread throughout the backcountry.

These jobs are geared towards young people, so they accept entrants with no experience whatsoever. These are some of the easiest to score and most exciting entry-level jobs you can find. In fact, I managed to get a baking and cooking job at the age of 20 through CoolWorks—with no culinary experience whatsoever. You can get practically any job you want, provided you demonstrate enough passion and reliability.

The jobs vary, of course, but the majority either offer free accommodation and food or a very cheap deal for both. Even better, a few of these jobs are willing to pay for your airfare to get you there! You could start with no money and find yourself spending a summer deep in the mountains of Alaska, hiking and rafting and flying around on tiny two-seater planes entirely for free.

In fact, that's exactly what I did. Craving adventure, I applied for all of the most remote jobs I could find on CoolWorks, most of them in Alaska. I was offered several, but ended up choosing one where I could spend the summer baking desserts and breads and pastries. After spending four months in the middle of nowhere, I came away with $9,000. And I had a brilliant summer. We had free lodging, free food, free flights anywhere in Northern Alaska, and free raft trips whenever we wanted them. I saw more bears and caribou than I've ever seen, and I even witnessed my first spectacular aurora.

This may sound incredibly lucky, but it's a situation common to many of these jobs. You're practically guaranteed to get a job, and you'll come away with more money than you would ever expect. In fact, my sister later used CoolWorks to get herself a job at Glacier National Park, and she used the money she earned to spend two months hiking in Patagonia the next year.

I like to think of CoolWorks as a baby step towards independence. You don't have much to worry about, since the company will provide for most of your needs, but you will get the chance to travel, earn money, and live on your own for the first time.

Of course, this experience could also serve as your first lesson in money management. Do you spend what you've earned on crappy beer from the closest town? Or do you save for the trip of a lifetime? Neither choice is inherently wrong. But it's better to learn the value of saving and budgeting before a botched job can cost you your home.

LAND YOURSELF THAT DREAM JOB

Here are a few rules for getting your very first **CoolWorks** job:

1. **Apply in January.** Most of the jobs are intended as summer positions, and applications open in early January. You have a much higher chance of getting the job you want if you're quick.

2. **Clean up.** The majority of these jobs have a zero-tolerance drug policy, so don't jeopardize your experience by making stupid choices.

3. **Go with an open mind.** My job in Alaska involved living in tents and spending the entire summer with just 35 people, and it was the best four months of my life. I was afraid the tents would be cold and uncomfortable, but it turned out they were huge structures with beds and wood floors, and when it got up to 85 degrees in midsummer, the heat was more of a problem than the cold!

4. **Be reliable.** It's very hard to get fired from one of these jobs, since finding someone to replace you at the last minute is a bit of a logistical challenge, but you do have to show up to work on time every day. Just do it.

5. **Expect to have the time of your life!**

One of the biggest perks of working in an awesome place is that you'll be surrounded by like-minded people. If you love beaches, choose somewhere in Hawaii and practice your surfing with the rest of the surfer crowd. If you're a fan of hiking, you'll have plenty of backpacking buddies if you spend your summer in Alaska or Glacier or Yosemite. And if you're a horse-lover, you can ride to your heart's content at one of the scenic Western ranches.

Many of your coworkers will, in fact, be disillusioned college graduates. Even after earning a degree, they haven't figured out what they want to do in life. And many of them have discovered they aren't the least bit interested in pursuing their field of study any further.

Travel with them, party with them, and learn from them.

And if you realize, at the end of the summer, that all you want to do is stay there forever, that's a valid choice. I know many intelligent, well-educated people who have realized their greatest calling is reconnecting with nature in one of the most beautiful places on earth.

Of course, after a summer doing your first CoolWorks job, you'll probably realize that, for the first time in your life, you have saved up enough money to travel. And that brings us to the next chapter!

Extra cheap travel for beginners

There are many ways to travel for almost nothing (or even earn money while you're abroad), and there's no reason to hold off on seeing the world until you've earned enough for the luxury package. In this chapter, I'll give you enough ideas for cheap, easy travel to keep you occupied until you're 50. From working holidays to WWOOFing, you'll find a cheap travel style that fits your personality and budget.

PLANNING YOUR FIRST WORKING HOLIDAY

Your first option for cheap travel is something called a working holiday. This is essentially where you are granted a visa to live, travel, and work in a country for up to 1 year (though the time limit depends on the country). Americans can receive working holiday visas for five countries: Australia, New Zealand, Ireland, South Korea, and Singapore.

This is a brilliant opportunity because not only will you get to live and travel in a foreign country for a year, you will be able to earn money while you're there. Even if you just work for five or six months, you'll earn enough to spend the rest of your time traveling.

Working abroad provides you a home base, which can cut down on travel fatigue, and it means you can leave most of your luggage behind when you go on short excursions.

Now, the easiest places for a working holiday are Australia and New Zealand. South Korea and Singapore have a very limited pool of available jobs, and Ireland only offers the visa to students. Australia and New Zealand, on the other hand, have a wide variety of entry-level jobs available at all times, and have many systems in place—such as cheap accommodation and easy-to-purchase cars—that help support the working-holiday crowd. In fact, towns such as Queenstown in New Zealand often seem to be populated entirely by Europeans on a working holiday.

Furthermore, Australia and New Zealand both have a very high minimum wage—$17 an hour and $15 an hour respectively! You can easily pay for accommodation and food and still end up with $500 a week to spend on travel. Australia in particular has a strong currency, so it's a good place to work if you're looking to earn a bit of extra money.

However, you must have around $5,000 saved (or borrowed) before you begin your working holiday. The first $1,000 is for your flight, and the rest you'll need to enter the country—proof that you can maintain yourself while you're there.

Here are the requirements for a working holiday visa:

1. You must be **under 30** (except in Singapore and Ireland)

2. You must have **enough money** to buy plane tickets and prove you can sustain yourself while overseas. $4,000 or $5,000 should be sufficient, though it varies from country to country. While some countries require these funds, they don't always ask for proof.

3. You need a **working holiday visa**. This does not take long to process online (only a matter of days for Australia and New Zealand), and is usually free or inexpensive.

If you've never traveled abroad before, New Zealand is one of the best places in the world to give it a try. The New Zealand travel industry practically babysits you—if you miss a bus you've booked, the bus driver will drive around town until they manage to track you down. Hitchhiking is still safe and easy in most places, and you'll be surrounded by other young travelers, mostly from Europe and Asia.

With a working holiday visa, you can earn more money than you would in the US, stay for a long time, and maintain a home base. It's probably *the* most straightforward way to spend time overseas.

FARMING FOR FOOD

Your second option for very cheap travel is **WWOOFing**, which stands for World Wide Opportunities on Organic Farms. Basically, small-scale farmers who need a few extra hands but can't afford to hire help will open their homes for WWOOFing, where you work a few hours a day in exchange for food and lodging.

Once you've arrived at the farm, you pay nothing until you leave.

You can pick whichever destination appeals to you and find a farm from there. Classic European choices include Italy, France, and Sweden. Who wouldn't love the idea of working on a vineyard in Provence or a honey farm in Tuscany?

One of the best parts about WWOOFing is that you'll be living with a family, so loneliness and homesickness will be less of an issue than if you embark on your first overseas trip entirely alone. And, if you're lucky, that family will treat you to some sightseeing while you're there!

The only consideration for WWOOFing is that each farm will require a minimum length for your stay. These can vary from one week to half a year, so choose your location wisely.

If you decide to look into WWOOFing, each country has its own WWOOFing database; once you've signed up, you will have access to contact details and descriptions for hundreds of farms. Choose the one that sounds best, and get in touch with the hosts through a warm, personal email. Your hosts will be looking for someone reliable and easy to get along with, not someone with a lifetime of farming experience.

I spent two weeks WWOOFing in Italy as part of a month-long trip through Italy, and it remains one of my most memorable experiences. My hosts took me to farmers' markets and medieval cities across Tuscany, and went hiking with me in the nearby mountains. It was the perfect way to save money and vary the experience, and I would do it again in a heartbeat.

Side note: in New Zealand, there is another good opportunity at hostels that goes by the name of WWOOFing or Work Exchange. In this setup, you help clean the hostel for a couple hours a day in exchange for free accommodation. It does not fit the traditional definition of WWOOFing, but it is another excellent way to save money!

OTHER ROUTES TO CHEAP TRAVEL

The two cheap-travel options mentioned above give you complete freedom to choose the job and location you want (provided you don't mind doing your working holiday in one of five countries). There are many other cheap travel setups that give you the freedom to find work or live inexpensively abroad; I won't go into these in depth, as they are usually more restricted options, but they are equally good ideas to research.

A few other cheap travel ideas include:

- Teaching English abroad—there are opportunities for this all over the world

- Working as a nanny in Europe—you can apply for an Au Pair visa in several countries in Europe that do not have working holiday options

- Working on a cruise ship—this will restrict your travel times and destinations, but you'll basically be visiting the same ports as the tourists, while earning money at the same time

- Volunteer work abroad (though be aware that many volunteer programs require a fee of several thousand dollars to participate)

- Couch-surfing—though you won't earn anything, you can stay free of charge when you line up accommodation with couch-surfing hosts

Whatever route you choose, know that travel is neither as expensive nor as intimidating as it has always seemed. You can earn more money abroad than you ever did back home, and have a wonderful time while you're at it! That will sound exactly like success to the very people who doubted you.

And finally, the next chapter will help get you started with planning your first solo trip. Once you've saved a bit, there's no better reward than to take some time off and see the world. Read on for tips that will give you the best experience possible.

Travel for the sake of travel

This chapter is for those of you who have saved a bit—maybe you've slaved away flipping burgers at the local McDonald's, or maybe you've done a summer CoolWorks job followed by a working holiday. That's what I did.

Anyway, if you're looking at this book saying, "I have a bit of money saved now. What should I do with it?", then this part is for you.

If you've spent high school working your ass off to save money, you deserve a treat. And there's no better way to figure out what you enjoy—what you really want—than to invest in a bit of travel.

It made all the difference for a young man I'll call Ben, who had gone through high school in a state of listlessness, locked away in his room playing computer games, apathetic about the idea of doing anything at all with his future. His parents were forever interrogating him about what he wanted, asking what he was planning to study. They suggested an endless roster of majors.

Nothing appealed to him.

Finally, Ben started traveling. He started hiking and skydiving and seeing his country, and from that moment everything changed. He realized that the sense of accomplishment at the end of a difficult hike was beyond anything he had ever experienced. Standing at the top of a ridge, confronted with a breathtaking mountain vista, was the greatest thrill he had ever known.

So Ben redefined his future. He began seeking outdoor programs, courses that would teach him to mountaineer and raft and perform wilderness rescues.

For the first time in his life, Ben had direction. He had found his purpose.

And you don't have to climb mountains to benefit from the eye-opening nature of travel. Another young woman spent a half-year in Europe and left completely enamored of London. She now lives in London, where she is constantly taking advantage of the theater productions and historic monuments and travel opportunities the city provides.

I too was changed irrevocably by my own travels. I had never felt at home while studying in Boston, and in my travels, I sought both novelty and a place that felt like home. Eventually I discovered that the people I connected with best in all the world were my fellow travelers. I felt closer to the people I met briefly in hostels than to anyone I'd known for the three years I lived in Boston. I even met my future husband at a hostel in New Zealand.

And I discovered that the job was not important to me; it was the people and the place. As long as I could live somewhere close to the mountains, surrounded by people I loved, I would happily take whatever job allowed me to stay. I am a writer and will always be a writer, but I have worked contentedly for many years as a chef. It is the ultimate job for traveling.

BABY STEPS

If you think you might be ready to embark on your first overseas adventure, you can start here.

For Americans, there are a few places that I call travel destinations for beginners: Europe, Australia, and New Zealand. Even if you have traveled abroad before, you may want to test out solo travel in an easy location. Australia, New Zealand, and most countries in Europe are easy choices, because they have a strong tourism infrastructure in place, most (or all) people speak English, and most of them are considered very safe.

If you're confident that you can handle a foreign language and want to venture somewhere that feels less familiar, go ahead. But if you want to dip your toes in the water and figure out what solo travel is like before attempting anything too extravagant, Europe, Australia, and New Zealand are excellent starting points.

ESSENTIAL EQUIPMENT

If you've done a bit of travel before, you might already have most of these items. If not, start gathering your supplies now! For successful international travel, you'll need:

- **A passport**. If you don't have one yet (or if your current one is about to expire), apply NOW. Passports take several months to process, and you don't want to be caught out without a passport when your flight comes around.

- **A photocopy of your passport and driver's license**. If you lose those essential documents, you'll be stranded unless you have a photocopy to act as backup. You should contact the nearest embassy or consulate immediately if you lose your passport; they will assist you in figuring out what to do next.

- **A good backpack.** Whether you use a proper hiking backpack or just a duffel back that you can carry on your back, you'll want something without wheels for the majority of your travel. Unless you have somewhere to stow your wheeled suitcase while you tour around the country, use something you can carry comfortably. You'll undoubtedly encounter more stairs, dirt paths, and long slogs across town than you expect, and a rolling suitcase will turn into a miserable burden at this point.

- **Comfy shoes.** You'll be spending most of your time on your feet, unless you're planning to hit up the best beaches in the country. If you can only bring one pair of shoes, always choose comfort over fashion.

- **A credit <u>and</u> debit card**—just in case you lose one. A credit card is always handy, because certain countries won't accept foreign debit cards. Make sure you bring cash as well, especially if you're traveling somewhere rural. Most cities have ATMs; some small towns don't. (Also, check ahead of time where you can withdraw money. In Japan, foreigners can only withdraw money at post offices; in New Zealand, American debit cards only work at the airport).

ADVICE FOR SAVVY TRAVELERS

Here are a few tips to help you get the most out of the experience. As with anything, travel has a learning curve. Expect the first solo trip to be difficult, and each one thereafter to be easier and more rewarding. But if you follow this advice, you can avoid some of the mistakes most new travelers make and have a smoother, more enjoyable experience.

Here are some quick tips to start you out:

- **Pack light!** It could save you hundreds of dollars on baggage fees, and you'll have an easier time getting from place to place. Trust me—if you're traveling on a budget, you won't want to call a taxi every time you get off the plane. You don't want to be lugging a suitcase twice your size around the London Underground.

- **Bring a good book.** Especially if you're going to a country that doesn't speak English, you'll want something to read. Even if you never, ever read in normal life, you'll need something to keep you entertained for the long hours spent in transit.

- If you can manage it, **don't bring a computer,** and keep your smartphone time to a minimum. One of the best parts of travel is meeting new people, and you'll miss it if you spend your time glued to a screen.

- On that note, **talk to people**. This is easier said than done, especially if you are quiet by nature. But it's incredibly easy to strike up a conversation with your fellow travelers—you can always ask them where they're from! On my very first solo trip, I hardly talked to anyone, and the loneliness was crushing. After that I learned to seek out conversations with my fellow travelers, and the difference it made was astounding.

- If this is your first solo trip, **keep it short**—a month is a good length to try it out. You can always extend the trip if you're having the time of your life, and if not, you can return home before misery sets in. Of course, it's a common practice for Europeans, Australians, and New Zealanders to travel for 6 months or a year straight out of high school, so if you take the plunge and decide on a longer trip, you won't be alone.

Side note: Most very young Europeans go to Australia or New Zealand for their "OE" (overseas experience), and vice versa, so if you choose one of those countries for your first solo trip, you'll be surrounded by people your age. Unlike your American peers, these people will think what you're doing is perfectly normal!

SWITCH IT UP!

When you start planning your trip and brainstorming places to visit, one smart trick is to **switch off**. While you're sitting at home daydreaming of your upcoming adventures, it's hard to imagine how easy it is for the novelty of a place to wear off. But after a few weeks, every mountain starts to look the same as the last, and the art galleries and cathedrals begin to blend together.

So switch it up!

If you've just spent a week boating down the Amazon, give yourself a cultural experience in Rio de Janeiro. And if you've been trying to hit all the major cities in Europe, stop for a day or two in the countryside. The whole trip will be more memorable for its variety.

On that note, don't pressure yourself to visit *every* iconic city in Italy or *every* glacier in Nepal. After a while, they all start to look the same. Choose a few that pique your interest, and spend more time enjoying the ones you do visit. Rushing from one stop on the itinerary to the next will do nothing but wear you out.

GREAT EXPECTATIONS

And finally, there are a few things you're almost guaranteed to experience on your first solo trip overseas. I mention these not to intimidate you but to reassure you that every traveler has been there. One of the most difficult parts of travel is that everyone who knows what you're doing will be jealous, so they won't sympathize with you if you're lonely or bored or just plain miserable. If you say, "I haven't talked to anyone in two days. I'm so lonely I hugged a sheep," they'll say, "Who cares? You're in *Ireland!* You're having the time of your life! You're not allowed to complain."

The truth is, everyone has good and bad days when they're traveling, and no one back home will be inclined to sympathize.

If you need a shoulder to cry on, talk to one of your fellow travelers. They've been there. They'll remember.

With that said, here are a few things you can expect from your first solo trip abroad.

No matter how independent or outgoing you are, expect to feel some degree of loneliness or boredom. Expect to get lost, to miss flights, and to mix up your bookings. Just remember— you'll find your way eventually, even if you don't speak the language, and you can always re-schedule your bookings. One of my most memorable travel experiences was an overnight bus to Edinburgh booked last-minute after missing a flight to Scotland.

Expect to push yourself past your limits. Expect to try things you never even knew existed, and expect to fall in love with places you'd never heard of before.

Expect to see the world differently, to shift your perspective and your priorities. Expect to be changed.

Realize that no matter what happens, it will all make a fantastic story later.

And finally, expect to start itching for more as soon as you're home. The world is out there, just waiting for you.

Now that you've learned about all the tempting, super-easy travel options waiting for you, the next section will give you a bit of career advice to get you on track—after high school or after traveling for a while or whenever you want. You'll learn how to settle on a major, how to score yourself a good job without going to college, and why it's better to get an idea of what direction you're headed in before taking classes.

SECTION 3

Advice for the Career-Oriented

Choosing the right course

This section is for those of you who are interested in seeking a career. You might not need to travel and get to know yourself better; you're ready to start investigating which jobs are right for you. You could be stuck between two majors, unable to figure out what on earth you want to study, or interested in looking for work that doesn't involve a traditional university education.

The best way to solve this dilemma is not to go to university and flounder until you settle on a major that doesn't require too many credits for graduation. In fact, the answer might not involve college at all.

You see, studying a subject and working in that field are often not the least bit similar. You have to get past years of theory and essays before you see any sort of hands-on training, if it happens at all. You can get a master's degree in philosophy, but no one is employing philosophers to sit around pondering the mysteries of the universe.

A much better route is to explore jobs that appeal to you, and choose your field of study based on what is necessary to secure that job. After all, if you go for the degree first, you might later learn you hate the job.

Most jobs are not glamorous. They involve the same work day after day, and if that routine work bores you or frustrates you to death, you'll never be happy there. Some people gravitate towards nursing because they love caring for people and making a difference in their lives. But if the idea of giving old people baths, turning them over, and cleaning up their diarrhea is something that you can't cope with, maybe you should steer clear of the field.

Likewise, book-editing is one of my fields of study and one of my greatest strengths, but going through a book word by word to fix the grammar and spelling inevitably puts me to sleep. Though it was a fascinating subject to study and a good match for a potential career, I couldn't force myself to do it for a job unless I had no other choice.

On the flip side, if you take on an internship or an apprenticeship in a field you hadn't considered, you might realize you love a job you have never imagined. I had always imagined myself working at a publishing house, but while I completed a two-year internship at a literary agency, I realized that literary agencies dealt with the aspect of publishing that interested me—working directly with books—while publishing houses were mostly concerned with marketing and sales and publicity. From then on, I changed my job search to focus on literary agencies, where I already knew I would be happy.

My sister had a similar experience. After studying environ-mental geography for several years, uncertain of which career path to pursue but considering field research, she spent a semester doing a field research course in Patagonia. Her 15-student class spent two months hiking through the mountains of Patagonia, researching the animals and trees and glaciers they encountered along the way. Once she finished the course, she realized that field research was not actually that interesting to her (though most people imagine field researchers to follow in the footsteps of Jane Goodall, she met one field researcher in particular who had spent the last 20 years of her life studying pollinators of the Ulmo tree, which most of us have never even heard of!).

Instead, she discovered that what mattered most to her was hiking and being in the wilderness—and advocating for the preservation of wild places.

Trying it out

However you do it, one of the most important things you should do when deciding on a career is *try it out*. After all, you might be devoting the next 20 or 30 years of your life to it. Most of us spend more waking hours at work than anywhere else. Just as you wouldn't marry someone without dating them first to figure out if you're compatible, you shouldn't invest hundreds of thousands of dollars in training for a career before you know it's something you actually want.

There are plenty of ways to trial a job and see if it fits. I'm only going to focus on the most common methods:

1. **Shadowing**
2. **Internships**
3. **Apprenticeships**

Everyone—even adults—should consider shadowing before they dive into a new job. But I've put this section first because it is something you can do as a teen, with no experience or credentials whatsoever. You'll spend a day or a week following a professional at work, which will give you an excellent idea what the job is actually like.

If you love the idea of helping plan trips but don't like talking to customers constantly, you might be discouraged to realize that travel agencies spend most of the day answering phones. Conversely, you might discover you love the fast-paced nature of working in a kitchen.

Whichever jobs you choose to shadow, you'll get a behind-the-scenes look at what the work actually involves. This might be especially enlightening if you're pursuing one of those mysterious jobs in an office building where people just seem to sit at their computers all day!

Getting the opportunity to shadow an employee is quite simple. While you might not be allowed inside a meat-processing plant or a top-secret government office, most professionals are quite happy to allow teens a behind-the-scenes look at their work.

First, look at the network of people you know—your neighbors, your parents' friends, your friends' parents, and your relatives. If any of them work in a field you're considering, give them a call or send a polite email asking if they are willing to take you on for a day or more. Afterwards, follow up with a thank-you message!

Before you go, do a bit of research. Learn about the company and the job, so you can ask informed questions and get the most from the experience. Another bonus of shadowing is that it can give you good contacts within a company. When you can address your job applications to someone you know, your chances of getting hired skyrocket.

Even adults who have been employed for a long time can benefit from job shadowing, especially if they find themselves in a role they don't like. Better to get the insider knowledge now, before you're so invested in a particular field that you feel stuck.

Internships and apprenticeships

This chapter will show you how to score career-oriented internships and apprenticeships, which are a perfect route to gain experience, score contacts, and build your resume.

INTERNS DON'T HAVE TO BE COLLEGE STUDENTS

When most people think of internships, they imagine college students or recent graduates interning at companies as a way to get a foot in the door. Of course, some companies never hire interns (such as literary agencies that rely on a constant stream of unpaid students to manage their workload), but it is often the best chance anyone will get at landing certain jobs.

While some internships do require a minimum of experience in the field, many are perfectly happy to hire young, untrained high school students. If you're interested in pursuing a certain job, landing an internship can do three things for you:

1. As with shadowing, interning can **help you figure out whether you actually want to pursue a job in that field**—with the added benefit of allowing you to experience the workload and responsibilities of a genuine job.

2. **Internships add a huge amount of credibility to your resume**. If you go with my publishing study example, it's *way* more useful for me to say I interned at

a publishing house for 2 years than for me to say I got a degree in literature. Internships are akin to apprenticeships—real-live job training of the sort you won't find at schools.

3. And most importantly, **internships often lead to jobs.** If you're hesitant about study, wouldn't it be nice to figure out what career you loved...and then get hired straightway, without shelling out a fortune on college? If you discover later that you need to get a few additional qualifications under your belt, you can always take online classes or go back to school.

The most important thing you can do is take your internship seriously. Even though you're not getting paid, this could be your entry point to the field you're pursuing. If you're not ready to show up on time and get your work done, do a bit of travel or a random CoolWorks job and get the novelty of independence out of your system before entering an internship.

When you start looking for an internship, you can reach out to people you know, or apply for the intern positions listed on a company's website. Keep in mind that, as with jobs, some internships are highly competitive. You don't need the most prestigious internship in the country—you just need one that will give you contacts and experience.

Note: Many volunteer positions have the same resume-building and job-snagging benefits as internships. After all, internships are just fancy (usually office-related) volunteer positions. So cast your net widely when searching for a post!

PRACTICAL APPRENTICESHIPS

Apprenticeships are along the same lines of internships—on-the-job training in a specific field of interest. Apprenticeships are not as common in the United States as in other places, but they are often far more reliable guarantees of future employment than a college degree.

In Germany, apprenticeships are the expected course most young adults will take. Germany has devoted a large portion of its economy to manufacturing, so the country has a high demand for electricians, mechanics, and other skilled technicians. It's a system that works—as part of their education, German students complete a paid apprenticeship. When they finish, they have a guaranteed job and the right skills to prepare them for it.

There are just as many opportunities for apprentices in the US; it's just not an option most students consider. But it is just as viable as pursuing a post-college job.

There are currently about 60,000 apprenticeships listed on the US Department of Labor website, which you can search by state and town. You can receive training as an electrician, a store manager, a geological surveyor, a nutritional trainer, a pet stylist, and much more. You would be surprised how many careers are open to apprenticing. You'll start being paid as soon as you take the apprenticeship, and afterwards you'll likely fill the specific job that you were trained for.

If you don't think you want to study, but you have some idea what types of jobs interest you, why not take on an apprenticeship? You'll get direct job training and a guaranteed entry into the field, and you'll earn money as you learn.

The problem with the American education system is that the degrees offered promote entry into a very limited set of job fields. Competition for those jobs is fierce, so there is no guarantee of employment once you graduate.

Taking on an apprenticeship circumvents this problem. Better still, some apprenticeships are willing to pay for you to earn any education credentials you might need.

STOP AND THINK

If you're thinking of pursuing one of the more obvious career paths (doctor, lawyer, engineer) simply because it sounds impressive, take a moment to decide whether you're doing it for yourself or for your parents and teachers. We have far too many lawyers in the US and not enough electricians.

In fact, as a professor, my mother spends much of her time convincing her students *not* to attend law school. It could be a perfect choice for some of them, but for most students, it's just the obvious answer. After they've earned an undergraduate degree in political science or ethics or psychology or any of those vague subjects that don't lead directly to a job, they'll probably have many well-meaning family members asking what they intend to do next. When they say, "Uh, maybe I'll go to law school, or something," everyone applauds their decision.

Don't let yourself fall into that trap—don't go to college just to take classes that sound fun, and then hastily settle on one of the obvious, well-respected career paths just because you can't decide what else to do. Nine times out of 10, the job won't be a good fit.

Instead, if you're stuck between majors or career ideas, get out there and experience the workplace you imagine yourself settling into someday. Maybe you'll decide it's not right for you, and seek out more fitting options. Or maybe you'll realize that your dream career doesn't require a college education after all.

Even if you do end up going to college, you'll be doing it because it earns you the credentials for the job you want, not because you think college is your only post-High School option.

STRIKING OUT ON YOUR OWN

And a final note—it seems that bright young people, now more than ever, are able to strike out on their own and succeed.

Yes, I'm talking about entrepreneurship.

If you're full of ideas but can't imagine fitting into a typical career, don't limit yourself. It's easier than ever to start a business. If it's online, you don't even have to invest money to get it off the ground. Of course, not everyone is suited to owning and running a business—it requires a high level of dedication and organization—but it is perfect for bright, independent, business-minded people.

This is just to say that if you know what you want, and you know it doesn't involve college, don't let anyone force you into their own mold. Young entrepreneurs are enjoying a level of success unknown by most of the hardworking generation that raised them.

You have to choose the direction that is right for you.

College is one direction you can choose from many, many options. Don't let your well-meaning parents and teachers steer you onto a path you don't want.

If they question you, remind them that Albert Einstein and Thomas Edison were both school dropouts! Remember, there are nine commonly recognized types of intelligence, and only a few of them are tied to educational success.

Now that you know all about the wide variety of non-college options waiting for you, the next section will deal with what could prove to be your hardest challenge yet—getting your family on board with your decision to postpone (or skip) college.

SECTION 4

Why this way is better

TO EACH THEIR OWN

Everyone is different, so there is no one-size-fits-all solution to feeling lost or directionless. If you're on the cusp of graduation, you're probably all too familiar with that fact.

In this section, I'll help convince you—and your parents—that skipping or postponing college is sometimes a better option for high school graduates than going straight down the obvious path towards a degree.

A NOTE FOR PARENTS

If you're a parent who is reading this out of an attempt to understand why your kids might be resisting the idea of college, go easy on them. This is a very difficult time of life, and pressuring them to attend college won't solve anything. Give them free reign to figure out what's right for them. Pushing them will achieve nothing but frustration on your part and misery on the part of your kids.

Winning approval

By this point, you might be fully convinced that one of these non-college routes is perfect for you. Unfortunately, only half of your work is done—like it or not, your parents are still a hugely influential part of your life, so your next job will be getting them on board with your plans.

Easier said than done. This chapter will give you a few suggestions of how to approach those difficult conversations with the people you love best.

CONVERTING YOUR FAMILY

If you're nearing the end of high school and think you might take some time off before diving into college, or even forego college altogether, here are some persuasive reasons why you *don't* have to go to college. The next time your family questions your decision, here are a few talking points that might help bring them around:

1. **"Think of how much money I'm saving you!"** Little though they might admit it, any parents who are willing to help their kids finance a college education are going to be hurting a bit for money. They've probably saved for years and will still have to pay a tidy sum out-of-pocket.

71

2. **"Wouldn't you rather I go to college later, when I'm more responsible?** If I go now, I'm probably going to skip classes and party hard, right alongside most of my classmates." Once you've gotten accustomed to your newfound freedom and decided you want to earn a degree after all, you'll be far more dedicated to your studies than if you went straight out of high school.

3. **"Everyone's taking a gap year these days!"** It's becoming more and more acceptable to take a year away from studies before college, so if any of your peers are planning a gap year, see if you can use their support to get your parents on board. (If you're intending your "gap year" to be more of a "gap lifetime," now might not be the time to bring this up!)

4. **"I'm building my resume!"** I know one young woman who applied solely for Ivy League schools and was rejected by every one of them. After spending a year traveling, interning, and working abroad, she returned... and got accepted into Harvard. She had won herself national attention when word of her adventures found its way into several prestigious journals, so the acceptance was an easy decision on the school's part. After she had finished high school with average grades and no hope in the world of getting into an Ivy League, she came away from her year abroad with a stellar resume that would recommend her anywhere.

5. **"I know what I want to do, and college won't prepare me for it."** If you're drawn to any of the typical apprenticeship fields, sit down and discuss your aspirations with your parents. When they know that you have an idea of what you're working towards, especially if it involves a secure, well-paying job, they'll be much more supportive of your non-college route.

6. **"I have no idea what I want to do with my life, and I don't want to waste my time taking classes until I have a better idea."** This last point is the trickiest, because your parents want only the best for you, and often that includes getting on the path towards a successful career and job security. Telling them you don't know what you want forces your parents to accept the fact that their aspirations for your future are separate from your own. They might have dreams of you winning prestige as a neurosurgeon or joining their ranks as engineers, while you might be perfectly happy to work as a nanny in France for a few years while you figure things out. Talk to them, and tell them you'll be able to earn money and live comfortably for a long time before you reach the point in your life when you'll want to settle into a career. If your parents care for you at all, they'll realize your happiness is ultimately more important than any superficial definition of success. If they don't see that, you would do best to strike out on your own before you find yourself trapped in their vision of your future.

UNEXPECTED PERKS

Apart from generally having a good time before college, you have plenty to gain from your time away from home.

First of all, you'll learn—and *earn*—independence.

That's more important than it sounds. When you move out, you'll suddenly realize how much you took for granted. You'll have to feed yourself, do your own laundry, figure out transportation (and all of its related costs if you decide to buy a car), pay rent, clean your house to a livable standard, and take control of your own budget. This is harder than it sounds. But you have to figure out these skills eventually, and the sooner you learn to cook for yourself and budget, the more money you'll have left for the exciting things.

One college freshman refused to help clean her dorm suite, saying "In my culture, our parents do the cleaning." Don't be that person. If you rely on your parents and roommates and eventually your partner to clean up your messes, you'll earn a lot of resentment from your more-responsible peers.

Secondly, you'll discover what truly matters to you.

Everyone is different. You might realize that you value luxury, and you'll redefine your goals to ensure you earn enough to live a comfortable life.

Maybe you'll discover that you're addicted to travel, and you want to see as much of the world as possible before you're chained to a job. You're willing to sacrifice a few comforts to see everything you can, and you're happy to pick up jobs wherever you go.

Maybe you'll fall in love with a place—a city, a state, a national park—and take whatever jobs allow you to stay.

Or maybe you'll find something you believe in passionately— like living a self-sufficient lifestyle; or guiding tours through an exploited, under-appreciated wilderness area; or rebuilding homes that were destroyed in a disaster.

Suddenly your life has purpose.

Direction.

Follow the goals that are most important to you, and you're sure to find meaning and happiness in your life.

Final words

I hope this book has helped you see that college is not the only option for you once you've graduated from high school.

Our society has focused so much pressure and prestige on college that our perspectives have gotten completely out-of-whack. A university degree is no longer the guarantee of employment it once was, and the cost of secondary education has risen beyond anything practical.

Everyone else in the world is incredulous when they hear how much an American college education costs.

Yet we keep shelling out money for often-useless degrees.

If you do go to college, first make sure it's the right option for you. Decide what you want for the future, and whether a university degree will get you there. College will always be waiting for you; the freedom to explore your options won't last forever. It's much easier to take chances and make mistakes before you have a house, a partner, and kids.

And if you decide college isn't for you, don't let anyone force you into studying. We need car mechanics and plumbers and cooks and hoteliers and builders to keep our country running smoothly, not more lawyers.

Let this book be your jumping-off point for your own post-high school journey. There is no career, no life, no version of happiness that fits everyone.

Figure out what you want, and the rest is easy.

Take this chance to make your future your own.

A note from the author

Please do not take this book as a dismissal of college! I earned a BA in writing, literature, and publishing (one of the fairly useless degrees), and I don't regret one bit of it.

However, I was enthusiastic about attending college when I applied, and my parents were very encouraging about the idea of taking a gap year or pursuing a different course. I had all of the options before me, and I chose college as the right course for my own interests.

This book is for those of you who don't feel as though you have a choice.

This is for the students who feel trapped by their parents' expectations, or weighed down by the peer pressure surrounding college admissions. This is for you if you're feeling lost and directionless. If you feel as though the only way to keep from becoming a disappointment is through following the conventional route.

This book is intended to show you that you're not alone, and that college is not a measure of past or future success—or intelligence.

So don't feel lost—there are thousands of students worldwide who have chosen to delay or forego college, and the vast majority of them have gone on to live happy, fulfilling, successful lives.

So go forth and conquer! And don't let anyone tell you what your future should look like.

About the Author

R.J. Vickers is the author of the bestselling Natural Order series; in her other life, she works as a travel agent.

When she's not writing, you can find her hiking, traveling, taking photos, and crocheting.

Though she grew up in Colorado, she now lives with her husband in New Zealand.

You can find her online at rjvickers.com.

Made in the USA
Middletown, DE
15 December 2018